The 30-Day Budget Challenge

Building a Spending Plan that Actually Fits Your Real Life

by

Tamra S. Connor, Ph.D.

Notes

For permissions, inquiries, or educator resources, visit:
https://www.tamraconnor.com

First Edition

ISBN: 979-8-950867-01-9

Cover + Interior Design: TnT WayPoints Creative

Published by TnT Waypoints Publishing, USA

TnT Waypoints, LLC is committed to empowering individuals and educators with practical, accessible tools that build lifelong financial strength, one intentional step at a time.

Printed in the United States of America

Notes

Introduction

Why 30 Days Can Change Everything

Most people don't struggle with money because they are irresponsible. They struggle because no one ever taught them how to build a spending plan that aligns with how real life actually works.

Real life is messy. It's busy. It's unpredictable. It's full of seasons, surprises, emotions, and obligations that don't fit neatly into a spreadsheet.

And yet, most budgeting advice still assumes you're a robot who spends the same amount every month, never forgets a bill, and never has a bad day, a sick kid, a flat tire, or a moment of "I'm exhausted, I'm ordering takeout."

This challenge was built for real people with real lives, responsibilities, and goals. Over the next 30 days, you won't be asked to become a different person. You won't be asked to cut out everything fun from your life. You won't be asked to follow a rigid system that collapses the moment life gets chaotic.

Instead, you'll learn how to build a spending plan that reflects:

- **Your values**
- **Your habits**
- **Your priorities**
- **Your rhythms**
- **Your actual life**

Not the life you *wish* you had, or the one someone else thinks you should have. You are focusing on ***your life***.

This challenge follows the TnT WayPoints journey that leads you through awareness, alignment, action, and adjustment. Your journey is a natural progression of real financial change. You'll start by seeing your money clearly, connect it to what matters, build a plan that moves you forward, and finally learn how to adapt that plan when life inevitably sends you down a bumpy road.

Each day includes:

- A short introduction
- An inspirational quote
- A simple, doable challenge
- An explanation of "Why it Matters"
- An opportunity to reflect

By the end of these 30 days, you won't just have a budget. You'll have a system that keeps pace with your life. You will have a sense of control that you may not have felt in years. You'll understand your money in a way that feels empowering instead of overwhelming.

And most importantly, you'll know how to keep going along your journey. You won't be perfect, but you can consistently make choices that support your goals.

This is your turning point. You have the chance to reset and build a spending plan that finally fits your real life.

How to Use This Book

Each day includes:

- A simple challenge
- A short lesson to help you understand the "why."
- Reflection prompts deepening your awareness
- An original inspirational quote to anchor the day

You can complete one challenge per day or stretch them out. What matters is consistency. This is your guide, your journal, your accountability partner, and your reset, all in one.

Let's begin!

Awareness

Seeing Your Money Clearly for the First Time

Your story opens with the realization that your money habits have been running on autopilot for a long time. It isn't a dramatic realization, just the quiet discomfort of noticing that your spending doesn't reflect your values. Days 1–7 will walk you through the emotional and practical awakening that comes when you finally look at the real numbers.

You will track your spending, identify the fixed and variable expenses, and begin to see the patterns you have been ignoring for years. You will begin to discover the leaks, leftovers, and habits that no longer match who you are. This first week is about honesty and the relief that comes with finally seeing the truth.

By Day 7, you are no longer overwhelmed by the numbers. You will be curious, engaged, and waking up to the realization that you can do this.

DAY 1
Track Every Dollar Today

Every financial transformation starts with one simple truth: you can't change what you can't see. Today, you turn on the lights.

You didn't mean to hit the "order now" button, but you did. You were tired. Work had drained you, and your refrigerator didn't have anything easy to prepare, so takeout felt easier than deciding what to make for dinner. When the confirmation email arrived, you just sighed. Not because of the food you had ordered, again, but that you couldn't remember how many times in the past month you had ordered takeout instead of preparing a meal at home, from the ingredients you had in your fridge, freezer, and pantry.

Today is the day you decided to start paying attention.

> "You can't build a plan around numbers you have never met."

The Challenge

Write down every dollar you spend today. Not to judge your choices, but to give you the data you need to start making changes.

Why This Matters

Most people don't have a spending problem; they have an *awareness* problem. You can't change what you can't see. Tracking your spending is the financial equivalent of turning on the lights in a messy room. Suddenly, everything becomes clear.

Budgeting starts with awareness. You can't fix what you can't see.

Today isn't about judgment. It's about honesty.

Purchase	Amount	Purchase	Amount

Reflection

What surprised you about your spending patterns today?

DAY 2

Identify Your Fixed Expenses

Avoidance keeps you stuck. Awareness sets you free. Today, you face your numbers with courage, not fear.

Today, you open your banking app and scroll through the bills that hit every month, like clockwork. The rent/mortgage payment, car insurance, mobile phone plan, subscriptions you don't remember having, and you realize that you have made money commitments you hadn't consciously agreed to.

Today, you begin to take control.

"Some expenses are anchors.
Other expenses are on autopilot.
Know the difference."

The Challenge

List every fixed expense: rent, insurance, subscriptions, and payments.

Why This Matters

Fixed expenses shape your financial reality. Seeing them clearly shows how much flexibility you really have.

Today is about bringing them into the light.

Fixed Expenses	Amount
Mortgage/Rent	
Car Payment	
Car Insurance	
Home Insurance	

Total Fixed Expenses	

Reflection

Which fixed expenses still serve you, and which are leftovers from an older version of your life?

DAY 3
Identify Your Variable Expenses

This is where your habits live. They create your patterns and highlight your impulses. Variable expenses are your opportunities. Today, you get honest about them.

Variable expenses are the unpredictable stuff in your life. Groceries, gas, coffee runs, and last-minute gifts because you forget about them in the hustle and bustle of your life. Variable expenses also include the "I deserve this" purchases. As you list them today, you feel a flicker of recognition. Your spending isn't wild; it is just untracked.

Begin to notice the patterns. And noticing is powerful. It's the moment when unconscious spending becomes conscious awareness. Today, you begin moving from unconscious spending to deliberate decisions.

You're building new awareness and habits.

"Flexibility is power,
but only when you know where it is going."

The Challenge

List your variable spending categories.

Why This Matters

Variable spending is where most budgets break. Naming your variable expenses gives you control. You are turning off cruise control on your journey to financial wellness.

This step is simple, but it's powerful.
It grounds you in reality and gives you a clear starting point.

Variable Expenses	Amount
Groceries	
Electricity	
Water/Trash	
Gas/Propane	
Auto Fuel	

Total Variable Expenses	

Reflection

Which variable category feels the hardest to manage?

DAY 4

Calculate Your Monthly Income

Is your monthly income stable? Does it change based on your schedule or other responsibilities? Do you have more than one job? Knowing your income is critical to proper planning.

Find your most recent pay stubs from the past 3 – 6 months. Add your income. It is probably more than you thought, and yet, it is never enough. However, it is your starting point. You can move forward from here with confidence in your numbers.

Knowledge leads to confidence.

"A budget built on guesses collapses fast."

The Challenge

Add up all income sources. Include the consistent dollars, the extras, the side gigs, everything.

Why This Matters

The income is the foundation of your spending plan. Accuracy matters.

Reflection

Does your income feel stable, flexible, or unpredictable?

DAY 5
Map Your Money Flow

Budget issues often aren't about the amount of money, but about the timing of income versus your expenses.

Tracking both income and expenses over time brings the rhythm of your money into the light. You can see when and where you need to adjust to have the funds available when the bills arrive.

You're learning about your money cycle.

"Money has a rhythm.
Learn the rhythm, and you learn control."

The Challenge

Using your bank app, write out when money comes in and when bills go out. Analyze at least 1 month of income and expenses; 2 or 3 months would give a clearer picture.

Why This Matters

Timing issues, not overspending, cause the most overdrafts and stress in our financial lives.

Date	Description of Transaction	Money Out	Money In	Balance	Notes

Reflection

Where does your money flow feel tight or rushed?

DAY 6
Identify Your Non-Negotiables

A budget isn't a cage, but it is a compass. To be successful, your spending plan must work with your real life, not the life some book tells you to live.

What are the things you cannot live without? It may be your gym membership or a weekend ritual with your children. It could be music lessons for your son or attending your daughter's softball games. What are the things that bring you joy?

Your destination is important, but more important is the joy you find along the journey.

> "A budget that ignores your real life will never survive your real life."

The Challenge

List the things you refuse to cut from your life. Identify the things that matter deeply to you.

Why This Matters

Budgets fail because they are too restrictive. Naming your non-negotiables helps you stay motivated to follow your spending plan.

This is about your values, not restrictions.

Reflection

What makes these items essential to your well-being?

DAY 7
Identify Your Money Leaks

Weekly planning keeps you grounded. It's where intention meets real life, one week at a time.

There's something refreshing about planning just one week.

Not a whole month
Not a whole year
Just seven days

It feels doable, manageable, and human.

As you sketch out your weekly budget, you feel a quiet confidence growing. You're not trying to predict the future. You're preparing for it. You're not trying to control everything, just the next few steps.

And that's enough. In fact, it is more than enough.

It's progress.

"Small weekly plans prevent big monthly problems."

The Challenge

Create a one-week spending plan based on your income and expenses. If you are paid bi-weekly or semi-monthly, create a spending plan for the period of time between your paychecks, if you prefer.

Why This Matters

Monthly budgets are great, but weekly budgets are practical. They keep you grounded, flexible, and aware of what's happening right now, and not 30 days from now.

Weekly budgeting helps you course-correct quickly, rather than waiting until the end of the month to realize you overspent.

Reflection

What feels realistic for this week?

DAY 8

Review Your Subscriptions

Tiny leaks drain big goals. Today, you plug holes and reclaim your money.

You didn't expect today to feel emotional, but it does. As you scroll through your subscriptions, you see the ghosts of past seasons. You see the workout app you swore you'd use, the streaming service you forgot you had, the free trial that quietly became a monthly bill. Each one is a tiny reminder of a moment when you meant well but didn't follow through.

But instead of feeling guilty, you feel . . . ready. Ready to release what no longer serves you. Ready to stop paying for things you don't use. Ready to reclaim the money you didn't even realize you were losing.

Canceling a subscription may feel small.

Today, you reclaim your power.

"Every dollar you reclaim is a dollar you can redirect toward your goals."

The Challenge

List every subscription you pay for, including streaming, apps, memberships, and renewals. Now cancel at least one.

Why This Matters

Subscriptions are the silent budget killers. They're designed to be forgotten. Companies count on you not to notice and keep paying month after month.

Canceling one subscription won't change your life, but the mindset shift will.

Subscription	Amount
Netflix	
Hulu	
Uber One	
Gym Membership	

Total Subscriptions	

Reflection

Which subscription was easiest to cancel? Which one surprised you?

DAY 9

Check Your Credit Score

Your credit score is a snapshot of your financial habits. Today, you look at it with clarity, not judgment.

You check your credit score with the same energy you'd use to peek through your fingers during a scary movie, with a little curiosity, caution, and while slightly braced for impact. But when the number appears, something surprising happens and you don't spiral. You don't judge yourself. You don't compare. You just . . . observe.

It's a number, not a verdict. A simple snapshot, not your final destiny. And for the first time, you see it as information. Not as your identity.

You're learning to separate your worth from your wallet.

> "Knowledge is leverage.
> The more you know,
> the better decisions you make."

The Challenge

Look up your current credit score.

Why This Matters

Your credit score is a financial passport. It affects your interest rates, insurance premiums, housing options, and sometimes even job opportunities.

Knowing your score isn't about judgment, but it is about awareness.

You can't improve what you don't acknowledge.

Reflection

What's helping your score? What's hurting it?

DAY 10

Review Your Credit Report

Your credit report tells your financial story. Today, you read it with fresh eyes and full ownership.

Your credit report reads like a timeline of your life, the apartment you moved into when everything felt new, the credit card you opened during a stressful season, the loan you took when you needed help. Some entries make you smile. Others make you wince.

But as you read, you realize something important: You've survived every chapter.

Your past decisions do not define you. You're informed by them.

And today, you're choosing to write the next chapter with intention.

Big changes begin with a first step.

"Your credit report is a story,
and you have the power to edit it."

The Challenge

Read your full credit report from all three bureaus.

Why This Matters

Credit reports contain errors more often than people realize, and those errors can cost you money. Reviewing your report is an act of financial self-protection.

This is your chance to correct mistakes, catch fraud, and understand the story your credit history is telling.

It is your chance to take the necessary steps to rewrite your future.

Reflection

Did anything surprise you or need correction?

Awareness to Alignment

Awareness asks you to look honestly at where you are, not where you meant to be or where you think you "should" be. Awareness is just your truth of right now. Awareness of your habits, your patterns, and your money story as it actually shows up in your daily life.

By now, you've seen things you used to overlook. You've named expenses you forgot you were carrying. You've noticed choices that help you and choices that quietly drain you. That clarity is your first real turning point. Because once you see your financial life clearly, you can finally decide what deserves to stay, and that's where you're headed next.

Alignment is the moment you stop reacting and start choosing. It's where you take everything you've noticed, including the helpful, the messy, the surprising, and begin sorting it against the life you actually want. Awareness shows you the map. Alignment helps you choose the direction.

Reflection

What truth about your current financial habits feels most important to carry with you into Alignment? And how might it shape the choices you make next?

Alignment

Decide what matters. Choose your direction.

Days 11 – 17 shift from awareness to intention. Setting goals, choosing strategies, and aligning actions with values become your focus for the week.

Awareness showed you the truth. Alignment is about deciding what to do with it.

This is the phase where you stop letting your habits run the show and start choosing what actually fits the life you want to build. Alignment isn't about perfection or overnight change. It's about making sure your money, your values, and your daily decisions are all aligned.

You've already uncovered what's been working for you, and what hasn't worked. Now you get to sort through it with intention. What deserves to stay? What needs to shift? What no longer matches who you are becoming?

Alignment is the moment you take ownership of your path. It's where clarity becomes direction on your journey to financial wellness.

Let's start shaping your next steps with purpose.

By Day 17, you will have done something powerful.

You've chosen. You've named your goals. You've identified your patterns. You've set your direction. And with that clarity comes a new kind of energy, the kind that makes you want to move.

You're no longer wandering. You're walking with purpose. And now that you know where you're going, it's time to take the steps that will get you there.

This is where the work begins, not the heavy kind, but the steady kind. The kind that builds momentum. The kind of work that builds confidence.

The kind that changes your life.

Notes

DAY 11
Calculate Your Total Debt

Debt feels heavy until you name it. Today, you take back your power by facing the full picture.

There's a moment, right before you total the numbers, when your stomach tightens. You already know the debt exists. You've felt it in the background like a low hum. But seeing the full amount on paper feels like turning toward a shadow you've avoided.

And yet, when the number finally stares back at you, something unexpected happens. It is a sense of relief. Because now you know. Now it's real. Now it's something you can work with.

The unknown was heavier than the truth.

"Debt is loud in your mind
until you quiet it with a plan."

The Challenge

List every debt you owe, including credit cards, loans, medical bills, and personal loans, everything. Now, calculate the total.

Why This Matters

Debt feels overwhelming when it's foggy. But when you put it on paper, it becomes a plan. Seeing the full number can be uncomfortable, but discomfort is often the doorway to change.

Debt loses its power the moment you face it.

Debt	Amount	Interest Rate

Total Debt		

Reflection

How did it feel to see your total debt in one place?

DAY 12

Choose a Payoff Strategy

Momentum or math, either will work. Today, you choose the strategy that keeps you moving forward.

You look at your debt list again, this time with a different energy. You're no longer standing at the base of a mountain wondering how to climb it. You're choosing your path, not with dread, but with strategy.

Snowball

Avalanche

Motivation

Math

There's no wrong answer. Pick the strategy that keeps you moving.

Today, you stop reacting to your debt and start directing it.

"A plan turns fear into focus."

The Challenge

Choose one strategy to guide your debt payoff

- Snowball (smallest balance first)
- Avalanche (highest interest first)

Why This Matters

A strategy gives you direction. It turns random payments into intentional progress. Snowball builds motivation. Avalanche saves money. Neither is wrong, and the best method is the one you'll stick with.

How the Debt Payoff Strategies Work

Start by checking your budget to see the total amount you can pay towards your debt each month.

Add all your minimum payments to find out how much you are required to pay each month.

If there is more available than the minimum payment amount, add all the extra to your first priority payment.

Snowball Strategy

Core idea: You pay off debts from ***the smallest balance to the largest balance***, no matter the interest rate.

How it works:

- Rank your debts by payoff priority (smallest to largest debt).
- Make minimum payments on all debts.
- Next, put every extra dollar toward the **smallest** debt.

- When that debt is gone, roll its old payment into the next-smallest debt.
- Repeat until all debts are eliminated.

Avalanche Strategy

Core idea: You pay off debts from ***the highest interest rate to the lowest interest rate***, regardless of balance.

How it works:

- Make minimum payments on all debts.
- Put every extra dollar toward the highest-interest debt.
- When that debt is gone, roll its old payment into the next-highest-interest debt.
- Repeat until all debts are eliminated.

Debt	Total Amount Owed	Minimum Payment Amount	Interest Rate	Priority

Reflection

Why does this strategy motivate you?

DAY 13
Set a Mini Emergency Fund Goal

Security starts small. Today, you build the first layer of your financial safety net.

You think about the last time an unexpected expense knocked the wind out of you, maybe you are remembering that car repair, the medical bill, or the broken appliance. You remember the stress, the scrambling, the feeling of being one surprise away from chaos.

Today, you decide you're done living like that.

A mini emergency fund isn't glamorous, but it's powerful. It's a promise to your future self: "I've got you."

And that promise feels like peace.

"Security isn't built in a day.
It's built one intentional dollar at a time."

The Challenge

Choose a starter emergency fund goal, typically $500 to $1,000, and commit to building it over the next three months.

Why This Matters

A mini emergency fund protects you from life's small surprises, so they don't become big setbacks. This is your financial shock absorber.

It is your first line of defense.

Reflection

What would having this cushion change for you?

DAY 14
Have a No-Spend Day

Today, you pause the spending autopilot and reconnect with what you truly need.

Today, you notice how often you reach for your wallet without thinking, out of habit, boredom, convenience, or emotion. You catch yourself mid-scroll on an online store. You pause before grabbing a snack you don't really want. You walk past a display that would've tempted you last week.

It's not about deprivation. It's about awareness.

And with every "not today," you feel a little stronger.

"Discipline is choosing what you want most over what you want now."

The Challenge

Spend nothing today. No extras. No impulse buys. No, "it's only $5."

Why This Matters

A no-spend day resets your habits. It shows you how often you reach for convenience, comfort, or distraction.

It's not about deprivation
It's about awareness

Reflection

What did you avoid spending today?

DAY 15
Review Your Spending Patterns

Your patterns reveal your priorities, even the ones you didn't mean to set. Today, you learn from them.

Looking back at your spending during the last two weeks feels like reading a diary you didn't know you were keeping. The patterns are subtle but honest. Those late-night purchases, the stress-relief snacks, the convenience meals on busy days reveal a pattern of financial decisions.

But instead of judging yourself, you feel curious. You're starting to understand the "why" behind your spending, not just the "what."

And that understanding is the beginning of real change.

"Your money follows your habits.
Change the habit, change the outcome."

The Challenge

Look back at your spending from the last two weeks and identify patterns.

Why This Matters

Patterns reveal priorities, even the ones you didn't mean to set. This step helps you understand your habits so you can shape them intentionally.

Reflection

What patterns stood out to you?

DAY 16
Create a Savings Goal

A clear goal gives your money direction. Today, you choose a destination worth working toward.

There's a moment today when you pause, really pause, and ask yourself what you want. Not what you "should" save for. Not what other people say matters. What *you* want.

A goal that feels Personal

Meaningful

Yours

As you write it down, something shifts. This isn't just about money anymore. It's about direction. It's about choosing a future that excites you instead of one that just happens to you.

For the first time, saving feels less like a sacrifice and more like self-respect.

“A clear goal gives your money direction
and your effort purpose.”

The Challenge

Choose one savings goal and set a deadline.

Why This Matters

A goal without a timeline is a wish. A timeline turns your goal into a commitment.

Whether it’s travel, a purchase, a sinking fund, or a dream, naming it gives it power.

Reflection

Why does this goal matter to you?

DAY 17

Automate One Thing

Automation is your silent teammate. Today, you let systems carry some of the weight.

You've spent weeks making conscious decisions, and today you give yourself a gift: one less thing to think about. You automate a bill, a transfer, or a payment, and it feels like setting a boundary with chaos.

It's a quiet kind of relief. A relief because knowing that even on your busiest, most distracted days, something in your financial life is still moving forward.

You're building systems that support the person you're becoming.

You are becoming the person you want to be.

"Automation is discipline
on autopilot."

The Challenge

Automate one financial task: a bill, a savings transfer, or a debt payment.

Why This Matters

Automation removes decision fatigue. It protects you from forgetfulness, stress, and inconsistency.

When you automate your priorities, you guarantee your progress.

Reflection

How will this automation reduce stress?

Alignment Spurs Action

Alignment is where your financial life stops drifting and starts pointing in the direction you actually want to go. In this phase, you took everything you uncovered in Awareness—your habits, your numbers, your patterns—and held it up against your values and long-term goals. Alignment asks one honest question:

Does the way you use your money reflect the life you say you want?

This section helped you identify what's supporting your future and what's quietly working against it. You clarified your non-negotiables, defined what "enough" looks like, and chose the behaviors that match the person you're becoming. When your spending, saving, and earning line up with your purpose, money stops feeling chaotic and starts feeling intentional.

And that's the point: Alignment sets the stage for Action. Once you know what matters and what needs to shift, the next step is to build the systems, habits, and strategies that turn your aligned intentions into daily movement. Action becomes easier, not because life gets simpler, but because your direction finally makes sense.

Reflection

Which part of your current financial life feels most out of alignment with the person you want to be, and what's one small shift that would bring it closer to your values?

Action

Build the habits. Do the work. Create momentum.

In Days 18–25, you will start implementing systems, making changes, and taking tangible steps.

This is the phase where clarity becomes movement.

You've seen your truth. You've chosen your direction. Now you begin building the habits, systems, and structures that support the life you want.

Action isn't about doing everything at once. It's about doing the next right thing, consistently, intentionally, and with a sense of purpose.

These days are practical
Tangible
Empowering

You're not just learning anymore. You're becoming.

By Day 25, you will have taken real steps, not theoretical ones, not "someday" ones, but actual, meaningful action steps. You've made decisions. You've built systems. You've created momentum.

And with momentum comes something new: awareness of what's working and what isn't.

You start to notice the habits that feel natural and the ones that still feel heavy. You see the progress you've made and the places where you still need support.

This is the moment when action evolves into refinement.

DAY 18

Review Your Insurance Coverage

Insurance isn't exciting, but it's essential. Today, you make sure your protection matches your reality.

Insurance has always felt like background noise, something you pay for but rarely think about. But today, as you read through your policies, you realize how much of your life is protected by these quiet little contracts.

You see gaps you didn't notice before. Strengths you didn't appreciate. And for the first time, you understand that insurance isn't about fear. It's about preparation.

You're learning to protect your future with the same care you're using to rebuild your present.

"Protection is a form of preparation, and preparation builds confidence."

The Challenge

Review your health, auto, renters/home, life and any other insurance policies.

Why This Matters

Insurance isn't exciting, but it's essential. It protects your financial stability when life throws the unexpected at you.

Today is about making sure you're covered. That you are not overpaying, and not under-protected.

You are developing a much-needed risk management plan

Type of Coverage	Insurance Company/ Agent	Coverage	Exclusions	Premium	Deductible	Policy Limits
Home						
Auto						
Life						
Health						
Disability						

Reflection

What did you learn about your coverage? What should you change?

DAY 19
Identify One Money Leak

Leaks hide in habits. Today, find one and fix it.

You spot it almost immediately, that one small habit that's been quietly draining your money. Maybe it's a fee. Maybe it's a convenience. Maybe it's a crutch. Maybe it's a vice you have been wanting to eliminate from your life. Maybe it's a pattern you didn't realize had become routine.

But instead of feeling frustrated, you feel empowered. Because now you see it. And once you see a leak, you can fix it.

Today, you tighten one bolt on the ship you're learning to steer.

“Small leaks sink big ships.
Patch them early.”

The Challenge

Find one recurring money leak. It can be something small that adds up, and then fix it.

Why This Matters

Money leaks are sneaky. They hide in habits, fees, convenience, and autopay. Fixing even one leak creates immediate breathing room.

Reflection

What leak did you find, and how will you fix it?

DAY 20
Create a Sinking Fund

Future expenses don't have to be surprises. Today, you can plan ahead to reduce tomorrow's stress.

You think about the expenses that always seem to catch you off guard. It could be the holidays, the car repairs, the school fees, or the trips you want to take. They're not surprises. They're just unplanned.

Today, you change that.

You choose one future expense and start preparing for it. And suddenly, the future feels less like a storm you must brace for and more like a destination you're planning toward.

You are building your life plan.

"Planning ahead turns
chaos into calm."

The Challenge

Choose one upcoming expense and start a sinking fund for it. Determine how much you need to set aside, each payday, so you are ready when the expense is due.

Why This Matters

A sinking fund turns future stress into future readiness. It prevents "emergencies" that aren't emergencies, just unplanned events.

Reflection

What sinking fund did you choose, and why?

DAY 21
Review Your Paycheck Deductions

Your paycheck tells a story most people never read. Today, you learn exactly where your money goes.

You look at your paycheck with new eyes today. Not just the final number, but the path your money takes before it reaches you. Taxes, benefits, insurance, and retirement are the hidden architecture of your financial life.

For the first time, you understand where your money goes and why. And that understanding feels like stepping into a room you've walked past for years but never entered.

You're learning the language of your own income.

"When you understand your paycheck, you understand your power."

The Challenge

Look at your paycheck and identify every deduction, including taxes, insurance, retirement, benefits, everything.

Why This Matters

Your paycheck is a roadmap. Most people only look at the final number, but the real story is in the deductions. Understanding where your money goes before it hits your bank account gives you clarity, control, and confidence.

This is about knowing the *true* value of your work.

Reflection

What did you learn about your paycheck, deductions, and net pay?

DAY 22
Set a 1-Year Financial Goal

A year is long enough to change your life. Today, you choose the goal that will lead the way.

You sit with this one a little longer. A year can change your life, but it's still close enough to feel real. You think about what would make the biggest difference. What would make future-you breathe easier, stand taller, and feel proud?

When you finally write down your one-year goal, it feels bold. A little scary. But also, exciting.

You're not just reacting to life anymore.
You're designing it.

“A year from now, you’ll wish you had started today. So start.”

The Challenge

Choose one meaningful financial goal you want to accomplish in the next 12 months.

Why This Matters

A one-year goal gives you direction. It’s far enough away to be ambitious, but close enough to feel real. This is your chance to choose something that excites you, challenges you, and moves your life forward.

Reflection

What is your one-year goal, and why does it matter?

DAY 23
Declutter Something and Sell It

Your home holds hidden value. Today, you turn clutter into cash and clarity.

— — —

You pick up an item you haven't used in months, maybe years, and you realize it's been taking up space in your home and your mind. Letting it go feels like exhaling. You feel more organized and ready to continue growing on this journey.

When you sell it, the cash is nice. But the clarity is better. You're learning that your environment and your finances are connected, and that releasing what you don't need makes room for what you do.

Today feels like a reset, inside and out.

"Letting go of what you don't
need makes room for what you do."

The Challenge

Choose one item you no longer need and sell it online, to a friend, or at a resale shop.

Why This Matters

Decluttering creates space, mentally, physically, and financially. Selling something reminds you that your home is full of value you've already paid for. Turning unused items into cash is a small but powerful win.

Reflection

What did you sell, and how did it feel to let it go?

DAY 24
Review Your Banking Setup

Your bank should support your goals, not slow them down. Today, you evaluate your tools.

You've spent weeks learning the truth about your habits, your numbers, your patterns. Today, you turn your attention to the tools that hold your money. As you look at your accounts, fees, and features, you realize something you've never fully acknowledged: you deserve better than "whatever bank you happened to open an account with years ago."

You deserve tools that support your goals. Tools that make your life easier. Tools that match the person you're becoming.

Today, you stop settling for default settings and start choosing with intention.

"The right tools make the journey easier.
Choose wisely."

The Challenge

Evaluate your bank accounts, fees, interest rates, and features.

Why This Matters

Your bank should work for you, not drain you with fees or limit your options. Today is about ensuring your financial tools align with your financial goals.

Reflection

What changes do you want to make to your banking setup?

DAY 25
Identify Your Money Strengths

You're doing more right than you realize. Today, you acknowledge the habits that are already working.

You've spent so much of your life focusing on what you need to fix that you almost forget to notice what you're doing right. But today, as you list your strengths, something warm rises in your chest. It may be pride or recognition that you have grown and are taking steps to preserve your own financial wellness.

You see the moments you made smart choices. The times you stretched a dollar. The discipline you didn't give yourself credit for. The resilience you didn't realize counted.

You're not starting from scratch.

You're starting from strength.

"Your strengths are proof that you're capable of more than you think."

The Challenge

List the things you do well with money, even the small things.

Why This Matters

Most people focus on their mistakes and overlook their strengths. But confidence grows when you acknowledge what you're already doing right. Strengths are the foundation you build on.

Reflection

What are your top money strengths?

Action Allows for Adjustment

Action is where your financial life stops living on paper and starts showing up in real time. In this phase, you took the clarity you built in Alignment and turned it into movement by taking small, consistent, repeatable steps to reshape your habits, your systems, and ultimately your outcomes. Action isn't about perfection or intensity; it's about building a rhythm you can actually sustain.

This section helped you translate aligned intentions into daily behaviors: setting up automations, creating spending boundaries that align with your values, choosing priorities, and practicing the discipline of doing the next right thing, even when it's inconvenient. Action is where confidence grows, not because everything goes smoothly, but because you learn you can follow through.

And that's the truth most people miss: taking action doesn't guarantee a straight line. Life shifts. Income changes. Emergencies happen. Motivation dips. That's why the next phase, Adjustment, is essential. Once you've been in motion long enough to see what's working and what's not, Adjustment gives you the space to refine, recalibrate, and realign without shame. It's where your plan becomes resilient instead of rigid.

Reflection

What is one action you've taken recently that moved you closer to the life you want, and what did it teach you about what needs to be adjusted next?

____

____

____

Adjustment

Refine.
Strengthen.
Sustain.
Become the next version of yourself.

In this final phase, you will evaluate, adjust, and prepare for long-term success.

Adjustment is where growth becomes identity.

This phase isn't about starting over; it's about fine-tuning. It's where you look honestly and compassionately at your strengths, weaknesses, wins, and challenges. It's where you refine your habits, reinforce your progress, and prepare for long-term success.

Adjustment is the phase that turns a 30-day challenge into a lifelong shift.

It's where you step into the next version of yourself. The one you've been building since Day 1.

When you reach Day 30, you will realize something profound: You didn't just complete a challenge. You changed your relationship with money and with yourself.

You're more aware
More aligned
More capable
More confident

And the best part? This isn't the end. It's the beginning of a new chapter, one you now have the clarity, tools, and confidence to write with intention.

Your journey continues from here.

DAY 26

Identify Your Money Weaknesses

Weaknesses aren't failures. They're opportunities. Today, you name them so you can change them.

Naming your weaknesses feels different now. They are no longer heavy or shameful; they are just honest. You've built enough awareness and confidence to look at your habits without flinching.

You see the patterns that trip you up. The emotional triggers. The blind spots. The places where old versions of you still linger.

But instead of feeling defeated, you feel empowered. Because now you understand them.

And what you understand, you can change.

"Awareness turns weakness into wisdom."

The Challenge

Name the habits that hold you back. All of them, including overspending, avoidance, impulse buying, lack of planning, everything.

Why This Matters

Weaknesses aren't failures. They're opportunities. When you name them, you take away their power. When you understand them, you can change them.

Reflection

What weakness are you ready to work on first?

DAY 27

Create a Future-You Vision

Your future self is waiting. Today, you imagine the life you're building and the person you're becoming.

You close your eyes and picture the version of yourself with steady habits, calm confidence, and a financial life that feels aligned rather than chaotic. You imagine peace, stability, and freedom. Today, for the first time, it doesn't feel like a fantasy; it feels like a direction.

You've spent 26 days learning who you've been. Today, you imagine who you're becoming.

And that vision becomes your compass.

"Your future self is waiting for you to show up."

The Challenge

Write a vision of your financially confident future self. Describe the life you want, the habits you've built, and the peace you feel.

Why This Matters

Your vision becomes your compass. When you know who you're becoming, your daily decisions start aligning with that version of you.

Reflection

What does your future-you look like, feel like, and live like?

DAY 28

Do a 10-Minute Financial Cleanup

Small tasks create big clarity. Today, you tidy up one corner of your financial world.

"Small steps create big clarity."

The Challenge

You tackle one tiny task today. A task that is something so small it almost feels insignificant. But as you tidy that corner of your financial world, you feel a surprising sense of clarity. It's like wiping a smudge off a mirror and suddenly seeing yourself more clearly.

You realize that progress isn't always loud. Sometimes it's quiet. Sometimes it's simple. Sometimes it's ten minutes.

But it counts. It all counts.

Spend 10 minutes cleaning up something small, deleting old emails, organizing receipts, renaming files, updating passwords, or tidying your financial space.

Why This Matters

Small maintenance prevents big messes. Ten minutes may not feel like much, but it builds momentum and reduces stress.

Reflection

What did you clean up today?

DAY 29
Celebrate a Win

Progress deserves recognition. Today, you celebrate the effort, the growth, and the momentum.

You look back at the last four weeks and feel something you didn't expect: pride. Not because everything is perfect, but because it isn't. Not because you did everything flawlessly, but because you didn't. Celebrate because you showed up, **again and again**.

Even on the days you didn't want to.

You've built awareness.

You've built habits.

You've built momentum.

Today, you let yourself feel the win.

"Every win counts.
Celebrate the progress, not the perfection."

The Challenge

Choose one win from this month. It can be big or small. Now, you need to celebrate it.

Why This Matters

Celebration reinforces progress. It reminds your brain that effort leads to reward. This is how habits stick.

Reflection

What win are you celebrating today? How are you celebrating?

DAY 30
Build Your Next 30-Day Plan

This isn't the end; it's the launchpad.

Today, you choose what comes next.

You have reached the final day, but it doesn't feel like an ending. It feels like a beginning, and it is. Today, you can start a new chapter shaped by clarity, intention, and confidence. You're not the same person who started this journey.

You're steadier

More aware

More capable

More in control

You choose one habit to carry forward. One milestone to pursue next. One commitment to honor.

And as you write it down, you realize something powerful: You didn't just complete a challenge. You changed your relationship with money — and with yourself.

"The journey doesn't end here.
This is your new beginning."

The Challenge

Choose one habit you want to continue and one milestone you want to reach in the next 30 days.

Why This Matters

Financial growth is a cycle, not a finish line. Today marks the end of this challenge and the beginning of your next chapter.

Reflection

What habit will you continue? What milestone will you pursue next?

Adjustment Melds into Achievement

Adjustment is where your financial plan becomes a living system instead of a fixed set of rules. After taking action long enough to see real patterns, you now see what's working, what's draining you, and what's surprising you. You have given yourself a great gift, permission to refine without guilt. You have permitted yourself to achieve financial wellness. This challenge was not about starting over; it was about responding to reality with clarity instead of emotion.

In this section, you learned to evaluate your habits, spending, priorities, and systems with honesty and curiosity. You identified friction points, celebrated what's sticking, and made targeted tweaks that keep your plan aligned with your values and your current season of life. Adjustment teaches you that progress isn't linear, and it doesn't need to be. What matters is your ability to pivot with intention rather than react out of frustration or shame.

And as you move forward, Achievement helps you recognize the milestones you've reached, the identity you've grown into, and the long-term stability you've built through every cycle of awareness, alignment, action, and adjustment.

FINAL REFLECTION

Your Money Story Is Changing

You've spent 30 days showing up for yourself. Thirty days choosing awareness over avoidance. Thirty days building habits that support the life you want.

This challenge wasn't about perfection. It was about progress, and you made it.

Now you know your numbers. You understand your habits. You've built momentum. You've proven to yourself that you can do hard things.

Your financial story is still being written, and you're writing it with more clarity, confidence, and intention than ever before.

Your future self is already grateful.

Reflection

As you think back on the past 30 days, what feels different? Not just the numbers, but also your mindset. How will you keep that momentum alive beyond these 30 days?

The Next Journey

You've just completed 30 days of showing up for your money, your mindset, and your future. You have a spending plan to guide you along your financial journey. That alone puts you in rare company. Most people talk about wanting change; you actually practiced it. You built awareness, aligned your choices with your values, took action that matched your season, and learned to adjust with intention instead of shame. That's real growth.

But this challenge was never meant to be a finish line. It was a doorway.

This book is just one in a growing series of TnT Waypoints Challenges. Each challenge is designed to help you strengthen a different part of your financial life with the same grounded, honest, no-fluff approach you've experienced here. Think of this as your foundation. From here, you'll move into focused 30-day journeys that help you build skills, confidence, and clarity one step at a time.

Upcoming challenges in the series will guide you through topics like:

- 30 Days to Debt Confidence: Understanding, Organizing, and Tackling Debt Without Shame
- 30 Days to Savings Momentum: Creating Systems That Make Saving Automatic and Sustainable
- 30 Days to Smarter Spending: Reshaping Habits, Triggers, and Patterns So Your Money Supports Your Values
- 30 Days to Financial Resilience: Preparing for Emergencies, Uncertainty, and Life's Inevitable Curveballs

Each challenge stands alone, but together they form a full roadmap—a series of waypoints that help you build a financial life that feels stable, intentional, and yours.

You've proven you can commit. You've proven you can grow. Now you get to choose your next waypoint.

Your journey continues from here.

Notes

www.ingramcontent.com/pod-product-compliance
Lightning Source LLC
LaVergne TN
LVHW040516210926
848480LV00005BA/1477
* 9 7 9 8 9 5 0 8 6 7 0 1 9 *